Ripley's Believe It or Not!®

Developed and produced by Ripley Publishing Ltd

This edition published and distributed by:

Mason Crest
450 Parkway Drive, Suite D, Broomall, PA 19008
www.masoncrest.com

Printed and bound in the United States of America

First printing
9 8 7 6 5 4 3 2 1

Ripley's Believe It or Not!
Remarkable Art
ISBN: 978-1-4222-3144-9 (hardback)
Ripley's Believe It or Not!—Complete 8 Title Series
ISBN: 978-1-4222-3138-8

Cataloging-in-Publication Data is on file with the Library of Congress

PUBLISHER'S NOTE
While every effort has been made to verify the accuracy of the entries in this book, the
Publishers cannot be held responsible for any errors contained in the work. They would
be glad to receive any information from readers.

WARNING
Some of the stunts and activities in this book are undertaken by experts and should not
be attempted by anyone without adequate training and supervision.

Ripley's Believe It or Not!

Dare To Look

REMARKABLE ART

www.MasonCrest.com

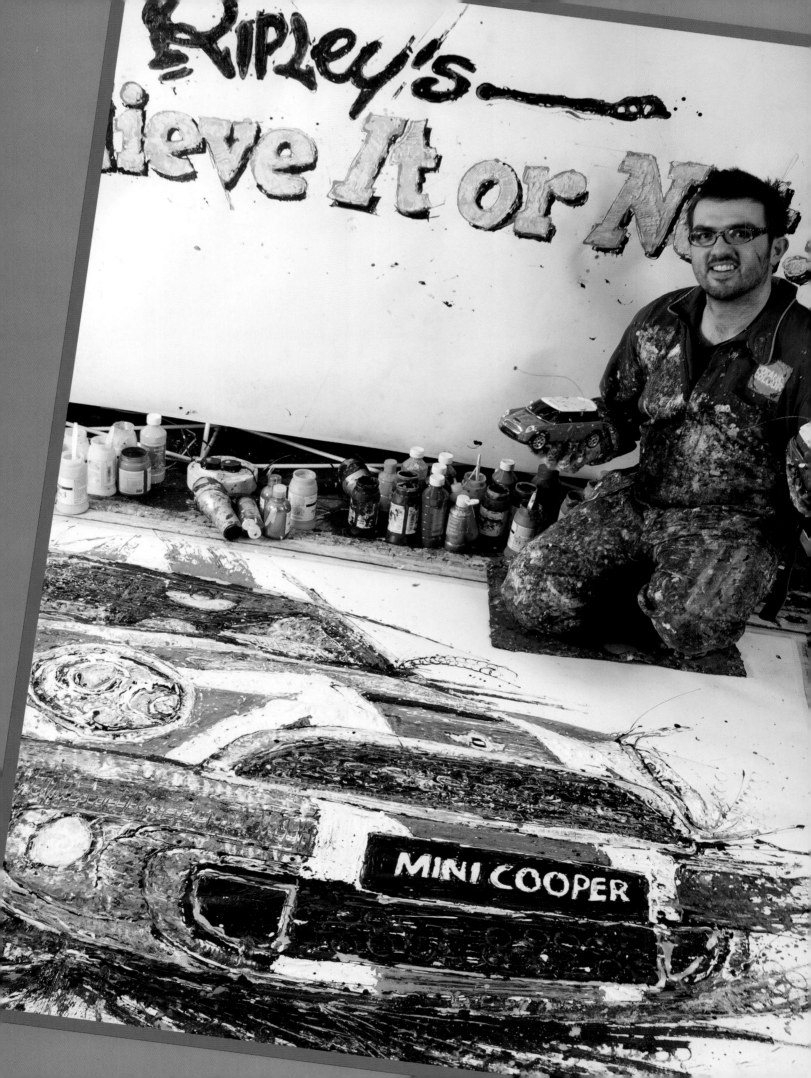

REMARKABLE ART

Clever crafts. Be amazed at spectacular sculptures and mind-boggling creations. Check out the hobbit hole made entirely of balloons, the creepy cakes, and the artist who paints with his own blood!

Artist Ian Cook from Birmingham, England, paints using remote-controlled toy cars and car parts...

BIZARRE BODY PAINT

In the bizarre world of 19-year-old Japanese artist Chooo-San, the skin on human feet is laced together, a belly has real buttons, and a zipper runs up the length of a person's back. It's enough to send shivers down your spine, yet she achieves these creepy creations without any digital enhancement—just by applying acrylic body paint to the naked skin of her models.

A student at Musashino Art University, Tokyo, Chooo-San (whose real name is Hikaru Cho) discovered her talent after doodling eyes on the back of her hand during study breaks. She developed this theme by painting a spooky extra pair of eyes onto a person's face or adding a second mouth in an unusual place.

Now she has gone even further, painting buttons and zippers on to friends' bodies to make it look as though they are literally bursting at the seams. Her artwork is so lifelike that the buttons, laces, and zippers actually appear to be attached to the skin.

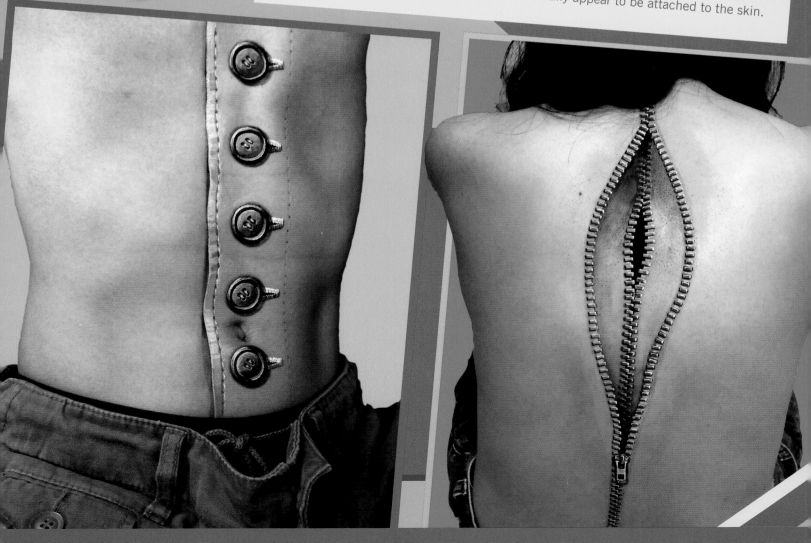

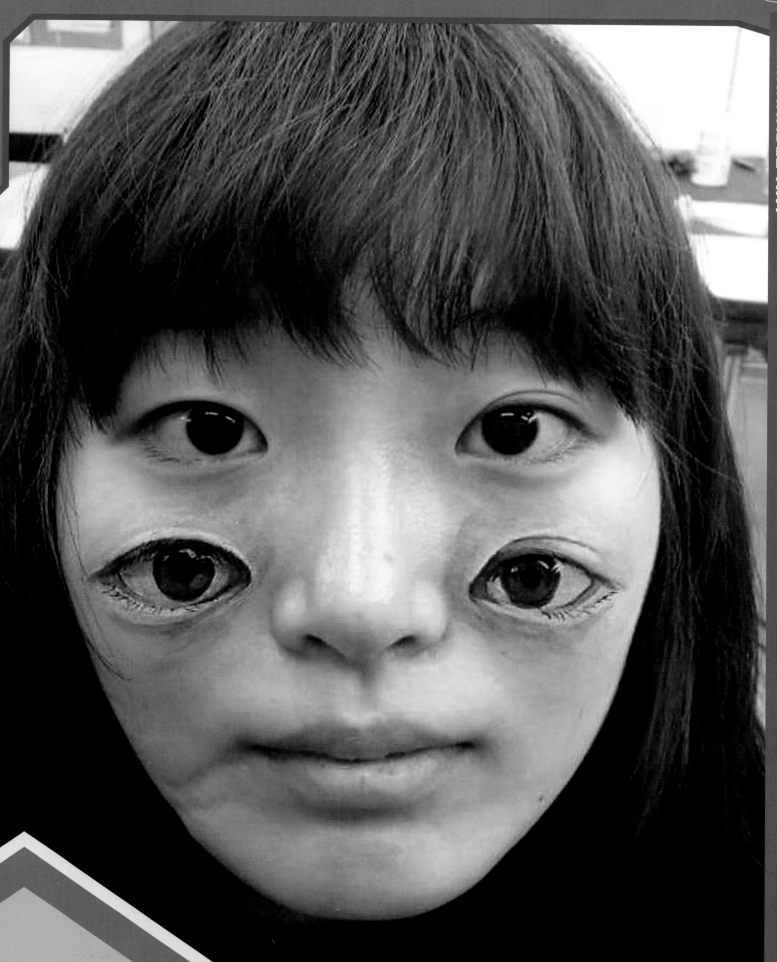

STREET ART

▶ In the summer of 2011, a row of condemned, dilapidated houses on Bellevue Avenue East in Seattle, Washington, were transformed for three weeks into some of the weirdest dwellings in America. Fourteen local artists were set loose on the empty homes and were briefed to convert them into a public art experience. Sutton Beres Culler used 12,000 ft (3,660 m) of bright red ratchet straps to tie two of the houses together, knocking holes in the walls in the process. Luke Haynes decorated one of the buildings with 1000 lb (454 kg) of old T-shirts. One of the deserted family homes was completely wrapped in household plastic wrap and fitted with a barcode, as if it were for sale. After three weeks the street of art was knocked down to make way for a new development.

BLANK CANVAS▶ In 1969, British minimalist artist Bob Law created a "painting" that consisted of nothing more than a large blank canvas with a hand-drawn black marker pen border and the date in the bottom right-hand corner—and it has been valued at nearly $100,000.

INVISIBLE EXHIBITION▶ The Hayward Gallery in London, England, exhibited 50 "invisible" works by people such as Andy Warhol, Yoko Ono, and Yves Klein for an exhibition of art that nobody could see. Featured artworks included invisible ink drawings, a piece of paper that U.S. artist Tom Friedman stared at for 1,000 hours over a period of five years, and a plinth on by Andy Warhol.

PAPER MUSTANG▶ Canadian artist Jonathan Brand has built a life-sized 1969 Mustang automobile—entirely from paper. The replica car started out as a 3-D model on a computer. Every piece of the digital model was then printed out on paper, cut by hand, folded, and then glued in place. The paper model is authentic down to the last detail, with a paper steering wheel, paper rear-view mirror, and even a paper engine housing paper spark plugs.

TINY DRAGON▶ To welcome the Chinese year of the dragon in 2012, Taiwanese miniature artist Chen Forng-shean spent three months creating a dragon sculpture that was just 0.5 in (1.2 cm) long—so small that it could fit on a coin and had to be viewed under a microscope. The incredible detail on the dragon included claws and whiskers.

▶ **AS A LABORER, FRENCH ARTIST PAUL GAUGUIN HELPED BUILD THE PANAMA CANAL.◀**

LITTLE LANDSCAPES▶ In March 2012, Kelowna Art Gallery in British Columbia, held a display of 4,154 standard postcard-sized (6 x 4 in/15 x 10 cm) original, landscaped-based works of art by local artists.

MAD HOMES • JULY 2011

723

115

115

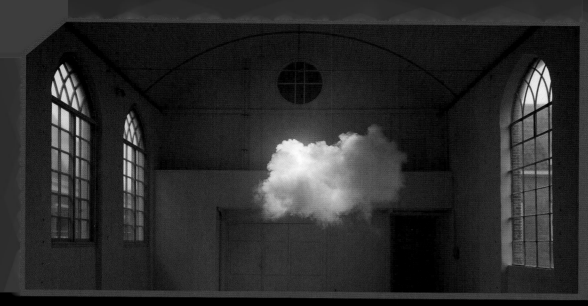

WEATHER OR NOT?

▶ Dutch artist Berndnaut Smilde's *Nimbus* artworks bring the weather indoors. His incredibly convincing homemade clouds, created with a standard smoke machine and water spray, are photographed in the few seconds before they dissipate, so the final images show the miniature clouds floating in empty rooms, as if by magic. No computer trickery or cotton wool is involved!

STREET WISE ▶ Michael Wallace uses his bicycle as a pencil and the streets of his home city of Baltimore, Maryland, as his canvas to create giant GPS images of assorted shapes, including an owl, an elephant, the Manhattan skyline, and a train. After studying the street map to see if any interesting shapes jump out at him, he plots his riding route, even if it means going the wrong way down a one-way street to finish his GPS artwork.

ART BATEAU ▶ A boat made from 1,200 pieces of wood, including fragments from Jimi Hendrix's guitar and the 16th-century English warship *Mary Rose*, was launched as part of an art project to mark the 2012 London Olympics.

STAPLE ART ▶ Artist Baptiste Debombourg created a huge, intricate mural in Prague, Czech Republic, using 450,000 metal staples.

ICE FESTIVAL ▶ Twenty-two truckloads of ice—some 440 tons—were transformed by 29 international artists into 90 Disney characters, including Mickey Mouse, Simba, Aladdin, and Buzz Lightyear, for the Bruges Snow and Ice Sculpture Festival in Belgium. To stop the characters melting while the festival was open between November 2011 and January 2012, the venue temperature was kept at 14°F (−10°C).

SPILLED MILK

▶ Christopher Boffoli, a photographer from Seattle, Washington, has captured popular food items in a bizarre new light. His miniature characters go kayaking in milk, mine for chocolate, and scuba-dive in cups of tea, among other daring activities. Christopher says that his humorous photos were inspired by the miniature scale toys of his childhood and America's food habits.

TWILIGHT ZONE

▶ Cathy Ward from Berkshire, England, is such a huge fan of the *Twilight Saga* series of books and movies that she has had images of the cast tattooed over her entire back. She spent £2,000 ($3,000) and 22 hours in the artist's chair to have tattoos of Robert Pattinson, Kristen Stewart, and Taylor Lautner inked on to her skin—and they were her first-ever tattoos!

TRUE FANATICS

■ **Peter Hygate from Kent, England,** has seen the original *Star Wars* trilogy over 300 times. He also had a *Star Wars*-themed wedding and named his two daughters Emily Rose Princess Leia and Bethany Violet Skywalker.

■ **Robert and Patricia Leffler from Wisconsin** have collected more than 4,670 items of *Conan the Barbarian* memorabilia since the 1970s.

■ **Steve Petrick from Pittsburgh, Pennsylvania,** has read each *Harry Potter* book over 100 times and has spent $13,000 turning his home into a Potter shrine. He also has four *Harry Potter* tattoos, including the Hogwarts crest on his shoulder and Sirius Black's prison numbers on his neck.

■ **Actor Nicolas Cage** is such a massive *Superman* fan that he named his son Kal-El, Superman's birth name.

LONDON TOUR▶ Leo Ihenacho (aka Leo the Lion), a former member of U.K. hip hop band The Streets, played 24 gigs in 24 hours in London, England, from July 11–12, 2012. Venues included the London Eye, a prison cell, and a meat market.

WASHBOARD MUSIC▶ Logan, Ohio, is home to an annual washboard music festival celebrating the use of laundry equipment as musical instruments.

PIANO PRODIGY▶ At age nine, piano player Ethan Bortnick of Pembroke Pines, Florida, became the youngest musician to headline a solo concert tour. After begging his parents for piano lessons, he started playing the piano at the age of three and was composing music by the time he was five. In July 2011, he headlined a show in Las Vegas, Nevada, at age ten, and has shared a stage with a host of stars from Elton John to Beyoncé.

MOBILE BAND▶ A three-piece Russian band, the Bremen Town Musicians, played a gig while speeding down a highway on a motorbike fitted with a drum kit and guitar amp. One member steered, one played guitar, and one played drums.

GUITAR TOWER▶ The Experience Music Project in Seattle, Washington State, features a 60-ft (18-m) tower made up of over 500 guitars.

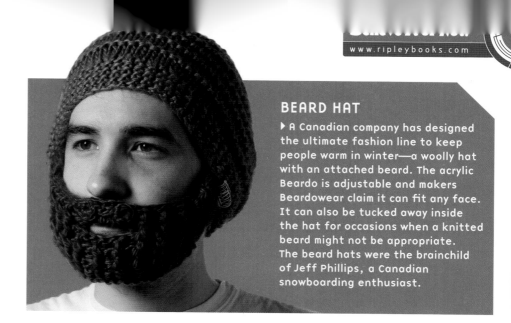

GUITAR SOLO▶ On May 14, 2012, David DiDonato performed a mammoth guitar solo when he played for 24 hours 55 minutes at the Red 7 club in Austin, Texas.

SHORTEST ANTHEMS▶ Uruguay's national anthem has 105 bars of music and is 6½ minutes long, while the national anthem of Uganda is only nine bars and lasts just 18 seconds.

DEAF DRUMMER▶ Scotland's Evelyn Glennie was the world's first full-time solo percussionist even though she has been deaf since age 12. She has learned to "hear" through her feet and often plays barefoot in order to feel the music better.

BEARD HAT

▶ A Canadian company has designed the ultimate fashion line to keep people warm in winter—a woolly hat with an attached beard. The acrylic Beardo is adjustable and makers Beardowear claim it can fit any face. It can also be tucked away inside the hat for occasions when a knitted beard might not be appropriate. The beard hats were the brainchild of Jeff Phillips, a Canadian snowboarding enthusiast.

LIGHTNING CONCERT

▶ *Wang Zengxiang is no ordinary electric guitarist. When he plays, a million volts of electricity surge through his body as he generates lightning bolts over 13 ft (4 m) long. Wearing special protective suits of metallic silk thread, which insulates him from the current, Wang and his band, Thunderbolt Fan, from Fujian Province, China, are rigged up to a Tesla coil, a transformer that acts as a giant lightning conductor. It produces vast amounts of voltage at high frequencies and creates spectacular bolts of electricity that arc through the air.*

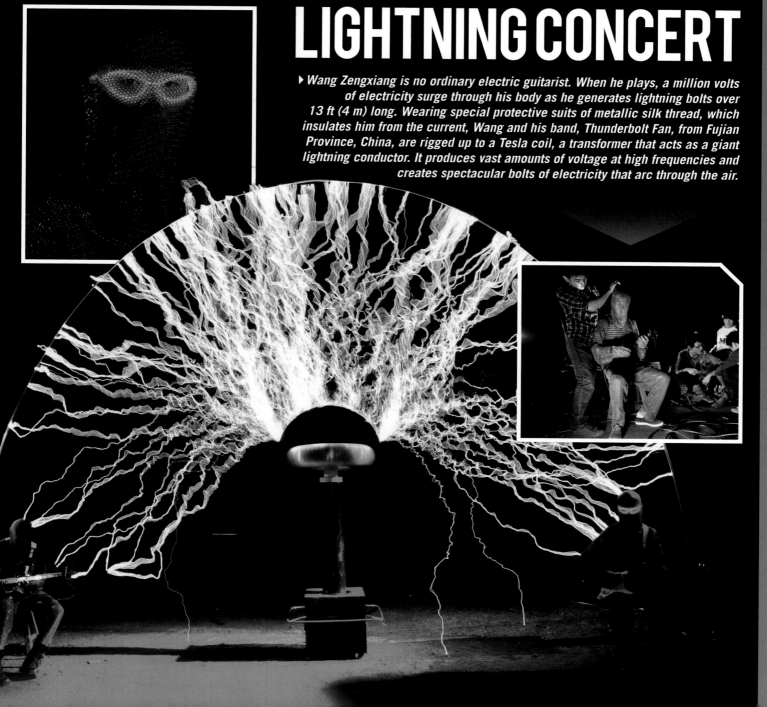

SEALED WITH A KISS

▶Japanese photographer Haruhiko Kawaguchi, like many artists, likes to capture couples in love. However, in his case he captures them in giant vacuum-sealed plastic bags! Although the concept may terrify some, all of his subjects, around 80 in total, volunteered for the *Flesh Love* project. Kawaguchi sucks all the air out of the large furniture bags with a vacuum cleaner and then has a matter of seconds in which to take his shots before the models start to panic. He says that while there have been no adverse effects, the men are genuinely more scared than the women, and he always keeps a supply of oxygen nearby for emergencies. Kawaguchi's methods are extremely dangerous and definitely never to be attempted at home!

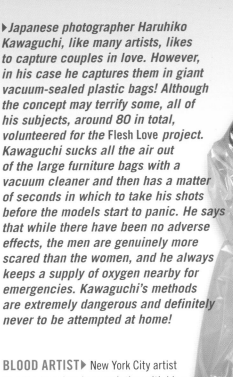

BLOOD ARTIST▶ New York City artist Nick Kushner has been painting with his own blood for 15 years. He says the pain he feels when drawing the "paint" from his body is cathartic.

LIVING ART▶ Belgian artist Ben Heine covers models in acrylic paint to create living works of art. He spent over three hours on each piece for his series called *Flesh and Acrylic*.

GALLERY BIRTH▶
Performance artist Mami Kotak from Norwood, Massachusetts, set up a birthing pool in a New York City art gallery and, as the culmination of her work, gave birth there in front of 20 people to a boy she named Ajax, on October 25, 2011. A video of the birth at the Microscope Gallery in Brooklyn was added to her exhibition *The Birth of Baby X*.

TALLEST TOWER▶ In May 2012, 4,000 children in South Korea worked together to build a 105-ft-high (32-m) LEGO® tower in front of Seoul's Olympic stadium—the world's tallest LEGO tower. It used over 500,000 LEGO bricks and took five days to construct.

CAR-HENGE▶ To celebrate the 2012 summer solstice, artist Tommy Gun created a replica of the ancient English monument Stonehenge using 18 scrap cars stacked bumper-to-bumper in London. It took him three months to build the structure that stood 16 ft 5 in tall (5 m) and weighed nearly 40 tons. It was designed to withstand a Force 12 hurricane.

SECRET SMILE▶ By turning Leonardo da Vinci's *Mona Lisa* on its side, New York City artist Ron Piccirillo claims to have spotted hidden, symbolic images in the 500-year-old painting, including the heads of a lion, an ape, and a buffalo, which he says show that the painting is actually a representation of envy.

SINGLE LINE▶ Singaporean artist Chan Hwee Chong has reproduced some of the world's most famous paintings—including Leonardo da Vinci's *Mona Lisa*, Johannes Vermeer's *Girl with a Pearl Earring,* and Vincent van Gogh's self-portrait—with just a single spiral line. His work is so precise that if he makes even the smallest mistake he has to start all over again.

STICK MAN▶ *Walking Man*, a 6-ft-tall (1.8-m) stick man sculpture by Swiss artist Alberto Giacometti, sold at an auction in London, England, in 2010 for more than $104 million.

DICE TRIBUTE▶ New York City artist Frederick McSwain created a giant portrait from 13,138 dice. The portrait was of his friend, Canadian artist and designer Tobias Wong, who died in 2010 at 35 years of age or, to be precise, 13,138 days old.

MILLION BEADS▶ In New Orleans, Louisiana, German-born artist Stephan Wanger used over a million recycled Mardi Gras beads to create the world's largest bead mosaic, measuring 8 x 30 ft (2.4 x 9.1 m). Titled *Sanctuary of Alegria*, the mosaic, which was completed in January 2012 after 14 months of work, depicted a view across the Mississippi toward downtown New Orleans.

ROYAL BEAN▶ Micro sculptor Willard Wigan of Birmingham, England, sculpted a portrait of Queen Elizabeth II on a 0.08-in (2-mm) coffee bean to mark her Diamond Jubilee. It took him four weeks and he painted it with a hair plucked from the back of a housefly.

PANIC ROOM▶ A bedroom at the Au Vieux Panier hotel in Marseille, France, is decorated half in white and half in bold graffiti. The hotel owner, Jessica Venediger, invited street graffiti artist Tilt to add bubble letters and tags on the walls, floor, furniture, and even the bed linen to create the "Panic Room."

ART BARBIE ▶

▶ French artist Jocelyne Grivaud has creatively combined the great paintings she admires with a childhood Barbie obsession to create these quirky and clever reworkings of famous masterpieces, starring the world's most famous doll. In this alternative art, Barbie takes the place of the mysterious *Mona Lisa*, by Leonardo da Vinci and Vermeer's *Girl with a Pearl Earring*. It can take Jocelyne days to prepare Barbie for a single photo. She says that the criticism of Barbie dolls inspires her to dress the doll up as iconic women in art.

MELON HEADS▶ Clive Cooper from Vancouver, Canada, carves human and animal faces from brightly colored watermelons. Each artwork takes up to six hours to create but lasts only a day.

BASKETBALL PORTRAIT▶ Malaysian artist Hong Yi used a basketball dipped in red paint to create an amazingly detailed portrait of Yao Ming, a basketball player who recently retired from the NBA team, the Houston Rockets.

TITANIC REPLICA▶ In April 2012, to mark the centenary of the sinking of the *Titanic*, Stan Fraser unveiled a 100-ft-long (30-m) replica of the ship in the backyard of his home in Inverness, Scotland. He spent 12 years making the 1:10 scale model, using two old trailers to form the hull.

TOWERING TRANSFORMER▶ Students at Hangzhou University, China, built a giant, 32-ft-tall (10-m) Transformer from discarded auto parts.

SLEEPING BEAUTY ▶
Ukrainian-Canadian artist Taras Polataiko staged an exhibition in Kiev where five young women took two-hourly turns to slumber on a bed at the gallery as the fairytale princess Sleeping Beauty. In keeping with the story, the Beauties promised to marry any visitor who woke them with a kiss, although the marriage pledges were not legally binding.

TONGUE PAINTER ▶
Ani K, a drawing teacher from Kerala, India, paints with his tongue. He was inspired to coat his tongue with paint and then lick the canvas after reading about an artist who painted with his foot. Ani first tried painting with his nose but found that his tongue offered greater control and he has even managed to grow immune to the paint fumes, which used to give him headaches and stomach cramps. He has completed more than 20 watercolors, including an 8-ft-wide (2.4-m) version of *The Last Supper*, which took him five months to paint.

KIT CAR ▶
To commemorate the Aston Martin DBR1 sports car that won the famous Le Mans 24-Hour Endurance Race in 1959, the Evanta Motor Company from Hertfordshire, England, handcrafted a life-sized artwork of the car in the style of an Airfix construction kit toy. Measuring 21 ft (6.3 m) wide by 11 ft (3.3 m) tall, the artwork shows the car broken up into kit form with the individual pieces affixed to a gray frame and is valued at £25,000 ($40,000).

COFFEE PORTRAIT ▶
Artists in Hawaii created a 16 x 25 ft (4.9 x 7.6 m) portrait of Elvis Presley—an image from his 1961 movie *Blue Hawaii*—from 5,642 cups of coffee, incorporating ten different coffee shades.

ROADKILL POTTERY ▶
Marion Waldo McChesney presses the mummified corpses of dead animals into clay to create unique pottery designs. Her artistic roadkill collection began more than 15 years ago when she found a frog—which she subsequently nicknamed Dorset George—dead but uncrushed in a Vermont driveway. She still uses George for her pottery impressions, along with a dozen other dead frogs, seahorses, starfish, lizards, and chopped-off bird's feet.

IMAGINATIVE ART ▶
Two New York City artists sold a piece of art that nobody can see for $10,000. Known collectively as *Praxis*, Delia and Brainard Carey founded the Museum of Non-Visible Art where, instead of purchasing a tangible picture, collectors buy an authentication letter and a small card bearing the artist's description of the work. Then they hang it on their wall and use their imagination to describe the piece of art to their friends.

HUMAN BODYWORK

▶ Here's a car with unique bodywork—made up of 17 naked men and women. The car was created by body-painter Emma Hack of Adelaide, Australia, who, working from a photo of a car that had been involved in a minor accident, covered her human models in shades of blue, white, black, and silver, to include alloy wheels and a license plate, before arranging the models in the car shape. She took 18 hours to achieve the perfect finish.

CLEANER'S BLUNDER ▶
An overzealous cleaning woman at Ostwall Museum in Dortmund, Germany, ruined a modern sculpture worth $1.1 million after mistaking it for a mess and scrubbing all the paint off it.

WORKING MODEL ▶
Louis Chenot of Carl Junction, Missouri, spent an estimated 15,000 hours building a 1:6 model of a 1932 Duesenberg car from scratch. He completed the model in 2010 and it has more than 6,000 parts, including an operational engine.

FINGERLESS EMBROIDERY ▶
Despite losing all her fingers in a fire as a child, Peng Jiangya from Yinjiang Tujia, China, can create intricate cross-stitch designs at a speed faster than many able-bodied artists. She uses her arms to hold and thread the needle and through hours of practice has perfected a skill that draws tourists to her remote village to buy her beautifully embroidered landscapes.

New York artist Vincent Castiglia has been painting with his own blood for more than ten years. He makes a preliminary pen or graphite sketch before extracting just enough "paint" in the privacy of his own studio. He describes his macabre medium as "liquid flesh" and his larger works take up to three months to create, sometimes fetching over $25,000. Human blood contains iron oxide, a pigment found in many paints.

BLOOD ARTIST

CREEPY CAKES

The world's most gruesome cake shop popped up in the Pathology Museum at St. Bart's Hospital, London, England. It featured such creepy confectionery as a bleeding heart perched on a wedding cake, a stitched-skin celebration cake, and cupcakes made using a range of toppings, including blood cells, maggots, severed body parts, lumps of flesh, and even stool samples.

The brainchild of Emma Thomas (aka Miss Cakehead), the three-day "Eat Your Heart Out" event graphically represented diseases and body parts in edible form. Many of the foodstuffs were so lifelike they made visitors retch. And what better way to wash down a blood-cell cupcake than with a stool-sample cocktail—a creamy drink made by James Dance using cocoa, strawberry syrup, and pieces of fudge?

Tongue

Hook

Flesh turret

GINGERBREAD HOUSE ▶ San Francisco cookie artist Curtis Jensen created an amazing scale model of Downton Abbey out of gingerbread. Curtis, whose past projects include a gingerbread model of Notre Dame, took more than a week to construct the elaborate Jacobean country house from the popular U.K. TV series using gingerbread, frosting, and colored candies.

WHO ATE BAMBI? ▶ Andrea Canalito from Houston, Texas, designed a sculpture called *Twinkle Twinkle Baby* made from giant cupcakes with the heads of baby deer sticking out from the top. The nonedible cupcakes took three months to construct from foam, modeling material, and paint.

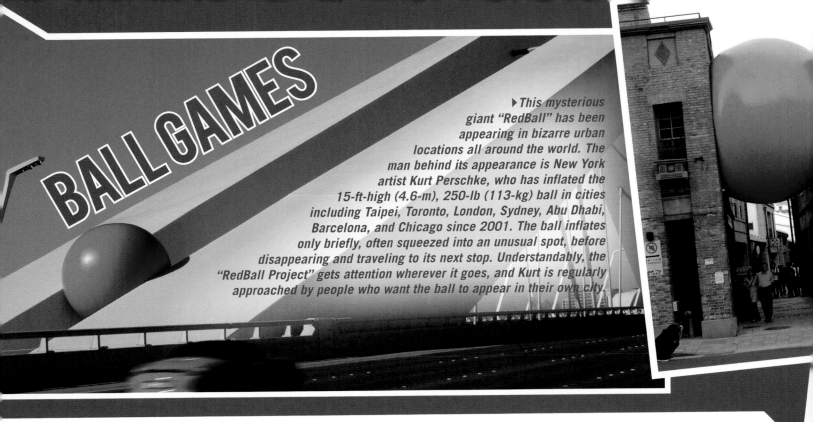

BALL GAMES

▶ This mysterious giant "RedBall" has been appearing in bizarre urban locations all around the world. The man behind its appearance is New York artist Kurt Perschke, who has inflated the 15-ft-high (4.6-m), 250-lb (113-kg) ball in cities including Taipei, Toronto, London, Sydney, Abu Dhabi, Barcelona, and Chicago since 2001. The ball inflates only briefly, often squeezed into an unusual spot, before disappearing and traveling to its next stop. Understandably, the "RedBall Project" gets attention wherever it goes, and Kurt is regularly approached by people who want the ball to appear in their own city.

PLAIN DOTTY▶ Nikki Douthwaite from Cheshire, England, turns the paper dots created by a stationery hole punch into celebrity portraits. For each picture, she uses tweezers and glue to stick up to 600,000 punched dots in a precise order.

CANDY MAGIC

▶ Los Angeles, California-based artist Jason Mecier has created this portrait of Harry Potter made entirely from black and red licorice! The sweet sorcerer forms part of Jason's *Licorice Flix* series, which also includes Willy Wonka, Freddy Krueger, Charlie Chaplin, and E.T. Licorice Harry is now hanging in Ripley's Baltimore Odditorium.

COIN MOSAIC▶ A total of 412 employees from a bank in Tallin, Estonia, teamed up to create a 215-sq-ft (20-sq-m) coin mosaic from 53,757 coins. The mosaic comprised 46,241 ten-cent coins and 7,516 five-cent coins, giving it a total value of 4,999.90 euros ($6,190) and a weight of 482 lb (219 kg).

GLOWING CORPSES▶ Japan's Iori Tomita transforms the corpses of fish and other small animals into glowing, luminescent artworks. He acquires the discarded carcasses from butchers and fish markets and chemically strips them down to the toughest part of their remains before dying them with bright colors. He has made more than 5,000 pieces since 2005, the biggest of which took a year to complete.

BALLOON SPIDER▶ Even though he is scared of spiders, balloon-twisting artist Adam Lee used 2,975 balloons to create a giant spider measuring 45 ft (13.7 m) wide at Grand Mound, Washington State. Lee has also created balloon versions of famous people including Barack Obama, Queen Elizabeth II, and The Simpsons.

STAIN PORTRAIT▶ Malaysian artist Hong Yi created an amazingly lifelike portrait of Taiwanese songwriter Jay Chou using nothing but coffee ring stains from the bottom of a coffee mug. She often uses unconventional media to create works of art, and has previously utilized sunflower seeds, chili paste, and basketballs.

WALK-ON SCULPTURE▶ The *Tiger and Turtle* sculpture in Duisburg, Germany, is shaped like a roller-coaster track but is designed to be walked and climbed on. Made from 99 tons of galvanized steel and perched on top of a mining waste dump, Ulrich Genth's sculpture is 721 ft (220 m) long and has 249 steps on the walkway, the handrails of which are illuminated by LED lights at night.

CAVE ART▶ Rock analysis of sophisticated drawings of bears, rhinos, and horses found on the walls of the Chauvet-Pont-D'Arc cave in the Ardèche region of France indicate that they are the oldest cave drawings in the world, dating back 30,000 years. The paintings depict some 13 different species of animal altogether.

TROUSER MOSAIC▶ Volunteers in Zhengzhou City, China, made a giant, 68,685-sq-ft (6,381-sq-m) mosaic from more than 23,000 pairs of trousers. It took over five hours to create and depicted an ancient Chinese cauldron and two Chinese characters that, translated, meant "fashion."

AUTO COWS▶ Miina Äkkijyrkkä, a Finnish sculptor, painter, and designer, buys dozens of used cars and then creates giant, colorful sculptures of cows from the scrap auto parts. Her love of cows began when she attended a dairy farming school in the 1960s and she regularly uses them as a subject for her works of art.

GROWING PICTURES▶
Zachary Copfer, a microbiologist-turned-photography student at the University of Cincinnati, has created ingenious portraits of Albert Einstein and Charles Darwin by growing bacteria in Petri dishes. He begins the process, which he calls bacteriography, by spreading the bacteria across the dish. He then places a photographic negative of his subject on top of the dish and exposes it to radiation, thereby controlling how and where the bacteria grows so that the image can be re-created in fine detail.

TOY DINOSAUR▶ The U.S. Space and Rocket Center at Huntsville, Alabama, is home to a life-sized T-Rex sculpture made from 160,000 pieces of K'NEX. The K'NEX dinosaur stands 12 ft 6 in (3.8 m) high and 33 ft 8 in (10.3 m) long, and weighs 10 lb (4.5 kg).

ATHLETIC BUS▶ For the 2012 Olympics, Czech artist David Cerny turned one of London's famous red double-decker buses into a robotic sculpture that performs push-ups. The six-ton 1957 bus, which Cerny bought from an owner in the Netherlands, is powered by wiring and suspension gear to move up and down on bright red arms, with each push-up being accompanied by the sound of a prerecorded groan.

AMMO MODEL▶ To comment on the role that religion has played in some of the major conflicts in history, California artist Al Farrow used gun parts and bullets to create a 6-ft-long (1.8-m) model cathedral.

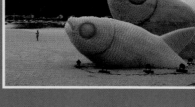

BOTTLE-NOSED

▶ Constructed from thousands of discarded plastic bottles, these enormous fish appeared on Botafogo Beach, near Rio de Janeiro, Brazil, in June 2012 to highlight the problem of plastics polluting the world's oceans.

PAPER CITIES▶ Dutch origami architect Ingrid Siliakus creates entire cities featuring New York-style skyscrapers by painstakingly cutting and folding pieces of paper. Spending up to two months on each cityscape, she uses no glue or adhesive, and calculates the spaces between the folded lines to 0.01-mm accuracy.

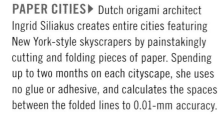

HOBBIT HOLE

Lord of the Rings fan Jeremy Telford built his very own Hobbit Hole—out of 2,600 balloons. It took the professional balloon artist 40 hours over three days patiently inflating each balloon with a hand pump to re-create Bilbo Baggins' house Bag End in the living room of his own home in Pleasant Grove, Utah.

By carefully twisting differently colored balloons into shape, he built a staggering life-sized inflatable replica of J.R.R. Tolkien's famous fantasy creation.

THE HOBBIT MOVIE

■ The first in a trilogy of movies, *The Hobbit: An Unexpected Journey* cost an estimated $270 million to make.

■ It is the first feature film to be shot and projected at 48 frames per second, twice as fast as usual. The higher frame rate helps to synchronize the images for each eye when viewed in 3-D.

■ Each of the 13 dwarf characters carries an average of nearly 176 lb (80 kg) of extra weight in the form of a fat suit, prosthetics, and a large amount of facial hair.

■ The dwarves' wigs and beards are made of imported yak hair, and in the course of the 18-month shoot, the production team went through 450 mi (720 km) of yak hair.

■ Each dwarf has six wigs and eight beards, knotted one hair at a time, to accommodate stunt doubles and stand-ins.

■ 5,000 prosthetic makeup costumes were constructed for the movie, altogether using 4 tons of silicon.

■ A typical goblin grunt is composed of 16 layers of sound elements.

■ More than 3,000 people turned up to a casting call in Wellington, New Zealand, where the movie was shot, in the hope of being chosen to play extras, forcing the police to cancel the call for safety reasons.

■ From a first print run of 1,500 in 1937, *The Hobbit* novel has now sold more than 100 million copies and has been translated into over 50 languages. A signed first edition fetched $90,000 at an auction in 2008.

■ Working as a professor at Pembroke College, Oxford University, England, J.R.R. Tolkien wrote the first line of *The Hobbit*—"In a hole in the ground there lived a Hobbit"—as he doodled to relieve boredom while marking exam papers.

LIVING DRAWINGS

▶ With just an ordinary pencil and a flat piece of white paper, Dutch illustrator Ramon Bruin creates 3-D illusion drawings that look as though they are jumping off the page. Using an airbrushing technique that he calls "anamorphosis," he draws incredible images of snakes, birds, and insects, and when he puts his hand on the pictures, he really brings them to life.

PIN MONEY▶ New York City artist Andre Woolery makes portraits of famous people—including rappers Jay-Z and Kanye West—from thousands of colored thumbtacks. He has also created a replica $100 bill from 23,850 green, silver, and black thumbtacks, replacing the picture on the bill of Benjamin Franklin with one of Benjamin Banneker, the 18th-century African-American scientist and astronomer most famously known for being part of the team that surveyed the boundaries for the original Washington, D.C.

SOCCER STUD▶ Using a powerful microscope, engraver Graham Short from Birmingham, England, painstakingly etched the full names of all 38 England World Cup goal-scorers onto a single tiny soccer boot stud. It took him six months to complete, as the slightest movement meant he had to start all over again. For that reason he wore a stethoscope so that he could engrave between heartbeats, and worked only at night to avoid the vibration from any passing daytime trucks. He has previously engraved the Lord's Prayer on the top of a gold pinhead.

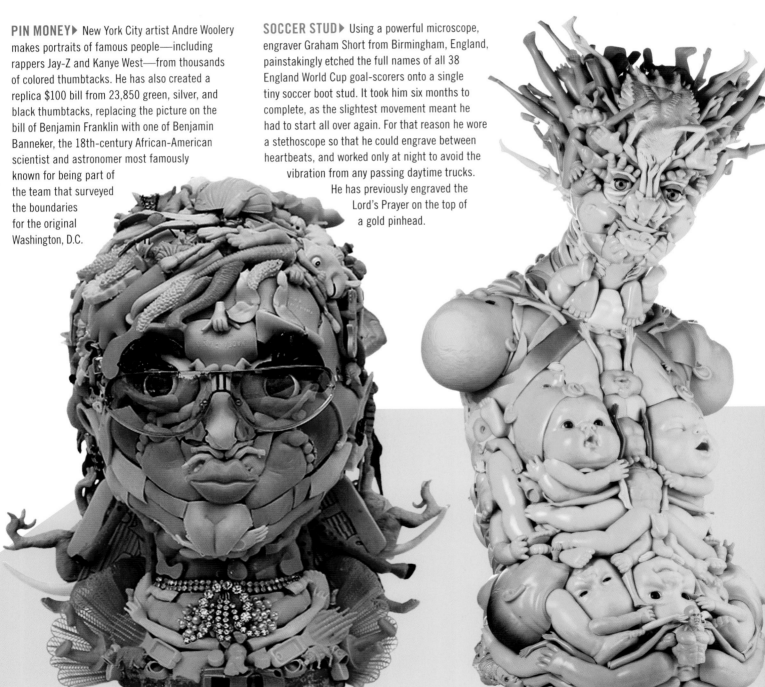

JELLY BEAN MURALS▶ Kristen Cumings of Martinez, California, re-creates famous artworks by the likes of Van Gogh and Vermeer using jelly beans. Each of her murals—some of which measure 4 x 6 ft (1.2 x 1.8 m)—uses around 12,000 jelly beans and can take her 50 hours to make. She starts by studying a reference photo of the artwork and then paints an acrylic version of it onto a blank canvas. Once that has dried, she begins applying the beans with spray adhesive, matching the colors to the original as best she can.

BEACH PATTERN▶ Instead of a brush and paints, Gunilla Klingberg used a modified tractor to create her patterned artwork *A Sign in Space* on a Spanish beach. A pattern made of truck tire treads was attached to a large metal cylinder and mounted on to the beach-cleaning tractor and when the vehicle was driven across Laga beach, it imprinted the star pattern in the sand. Whenever footprints destroyed the design, it was remade at the next low tide.

BANANA TATTOOS▶ Artist Phil Hansen from Minneapolis, Minnesota, has re-created famous artworks by Vincent van Gogh, Sandro Botticelli, Edgar Degas, and Michelangelo, using only a push-pin and a banana. He effectively tattoos the banana by spending hours puncturing the peel repeatedly with the pin, after which the banana skin slowly rots and blackens to reveal his intricate designs.

COOL STATUES▶ To create their *Street Stone* series, French photographer Léo Caillard and art director Alexis Persani dressed ancient sculptures at Paris's Louvre Museum in modern clothes. Caillard photographed the statues and then got his friends to model in identical poses but wearing skinny jeans, checked shirts, and Ray-Bans. Persani combined the two sets of pictures in Photoshop so that they merged seamlessly.

BLOOD ART▶ New York City artist Jordan Eagles uses animal blood collected from slaughterhouses as paint to make artworks as big as 32 ft (9.7 m) long. He uses fresh, decomposed, and pulverized blood to vary the shades and textures.

HENNA HURRY▶ Pavan Ahluwalia became the world's fastest henna artist when she painted a staggering 511 armbands in one hour at a school in Essex, England, on February 27, 2012. Each design was unique and she beat her previous record by a massive 131 tattoos. Once the henna is applied, it needs to be left to dry for around 20 minutes, after which time the henna comes away to reveal the intricate designs underneath. The self-taught artist has been practicing henna design since she was just seven and has seen her colorful creations used on hats, scarves, shawls, shoes, and even wallpaper and works of art.

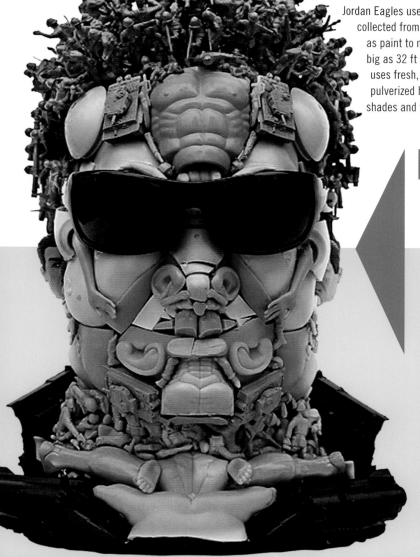

TOY
SCULPTURES

▶*Australian artist Freya Jobbins has created more than 30 sculptures of famous and imaginary figures out of recycled plastic toys. By painstakingly positioning each toy, she has built models including "Kerri-Anne," the Roman goddess Juno built from dolls' heads and Barbie doll legs, and a head of Arnold Schwarzenegger with "hair" made of toy soldiers.*

PUMPKIN ZOMBIES

▶ For Halloween 2012, a team of pumpkin sculptors led by Ray Villafane created a zombie pumpkin invasion at New York City's Botanical Garden. The Haunted Pumpkin Garden featured 500 spooky carvings of scarecrows, bats, bugs, spiders, and snakes as well as zombies. The pumpkins were sprayed with water to keep the sculptures fresh, but they became even scarier when they eventually started to decompose.

CHOCOLATE RECORD

▶ **FOUND**, a band and art collective from Edinburgh, Scotland, released the world's first fully functional chocolate record. The limited-edition chocolate disk, made by baker Ben Milne using the same negative metal templates involved in producing vinyl versions, can be played on any record player—but only about ten times before it wears down. The sleeve and label for the band's single "Anti Climb Paint" are also edible, made from rice paper and icing sugar respectively.

SAME SONG ▶ Alan St. Louis of Nashua, New Hampshire, performed the U.S. national anthem at special events 217 times in one year, singing for audiences as small as five at a college softball game and up to 12,000 at a New England Revolution soccer match.

JUSTIN BRIE-BER

▶ British food artist Faye Halliday has created a portrait of Justin Bieber out of soft cheese spread. She uses around three pots on each of her cheesy images, which also include Barack Edam-a, Marilyn Mon-zzarella, and Irish singing twins Ched-ward. She occasionally adds roasted garlic dip and sour cream and chives dip for extra texture.

DOG STAR ▶ In December 2011, canine actor Danny, a soft-coated wheaten terrier, retired after ten years of playing Sandy, Orphan Annie's faithful pet companion in the U.K. production of the long-running stage musical *Annie*. Danny, who joined the cast as a seven-month-old puppy, traveled the length of the country with owner and trainer Rita Mansell and notched up 1,400 performances, each rewarded with a dish of cheese and sausages.

ODD TITLES ▶ Contenders for *The Bookseller*'s Oddest Book Title for 2012 included *A Century of Sand Dredging in the Bristol Channel*, *The Mushroom in Christian Art*, and *Estonian Sock Patterns All Around the World*.

THE NAME'S BOND ▶ British author Ian Fleming was an avid birdwatcher and his fictional British super-spy James Bond was named after an American ornithologist, the author of *Birds of the West Indies*, first published in 1936.

CRAZY HORSES ▶ German designer Iris Schieferstein has created a range of shoes from dead animal parts, including high-heel horse hooves, sandals sculpted from deceased doves, and snakeskin stilettos with a replica pistol as a heel. She collects the dead animals from her butcher in Berlin, then removes the meat and bones from her chosen animal's foot before fitting the preserved skin, with the fur still in place, around a shoe model. Her shoes sell for nearly $6,000 a pair, and she has designed a pair of horse hooves for Lady Gaga.

ONE-TAKE MOVIE ▶ Indian filmmaker Haroon Rashid shot a 140-minute Bollywood thriller, entiled *One Shot Fear Without a Cut*, with a crew of 17 on a single camera, in one take, without a single cut. He rehearsed the action for five months before setting the camera rolling.

BLOOD COMIC ▶ A 1977 comic book featuring U.S. rock band Kiss was printed with red ink that had been mixed with the band members' blood.

BEATLES LOOK-ALIKES ▶ Each year the English city of Liverpool hosts a Beatles Week, which attracts more than 200 Beatles look-alike bands from around the world.

POLICE RESCUE ▶ Blind novelist Trish Vickers of Dorset, England, spent months painstakingly writing a book in longhand, only to be told one day that 26 pages were blank because her pen had run out of ink. However, local police officers were able to retrieve the missing words by using forensic technology to study the indents made by her pen.

KLINGON MASTER ▶ Even though he is dyslexic and had always struggled to read English, 50-year-old *Star Trek* fan Jonathan Brown of Milton Keynes, England, spent 12 years learning how to speak Klingon—and was so successful that he became the chief linguist on a CD teaching others how to master the alien language.

MIRACLE GLOW▶ Thousands of worshipers flocked to Saint Dimitrija Church in Skopje, Macedonia, in April 2012 after several frescoes of saints inexplicably brightened in color without being restored or cleaned. For years the murals had been blackened by the residue of candle smoke, but then suddenly—beginning with the picture of the Virgin Mary—the soot fell off them one by one in what churchgoers described as a "miracle."

POP (TART) ART▶ Tyler Kozar of Pittsburgh, Pennsylvania, won a million pop tarts in a contest and, after donating the food, used the packaging and wrappers to make works of art—including a 16-ft-tall (4.9-m) foil T-Rex dinosaur that is now on display in Ripley's Baltimore Odditorium.

MODEL THEATER▶ Eighty-two-year-old Cyril Barbier from Birmingham, England, has built a working model of a local movie theater in his bedroom. Fully lit, the cinema has a moving curtain in front of the screen as well as an organ that can be powered to rise up out of the floor and drop back down again. Meanwhile, a hidden DVD player plays movies on the 15-in (38-cm) flat screen, which is in perfect proportion to the theater's original 1930s screen.

ARTISTIC VANDAL▶ Polish-born Wlodzimierz Umaniec was jailed for two years in December 2012 for defacing a multi-million dollar Mark Rothko painting, *Black on Maroon*, at the Tate Modern gallery in London, England, by scrawling his signature on it with a black marker pen—and then claiming that the vandalism itself was a work of art. Repairing the mural will take up to two years and cost about £200,000 ($300,000), as Rothko's complex layering style mixes eggs, glue, and resin with traditional oil paint.

UNUSUAL SUSPECT▶ When the world's most famous work of art, Leonardo da Vinci's *Mona Lisa*, was stolen from the Louvre in Paris, France, in 1911, one of the suspects was Spanish artist Pablo Picasso. French police took him before a magistrate for questioning, but he was later released without charge. Ironically, he was in possession of a pair of Bronze Age Iberian statues, which had been snatched from the Louvre by a Belgian masquerading as a French baron, but the arresting officers never noticed the stolen artworks in Picasso's studio.

SHAMPOO PAINTER▶ Philadelphia artist Alex Da Corte makes paintings from dried shampoo. He often incorporates unusual materials into his artworks—past projects have featured soda bottles, Christmas trees and fingernails.

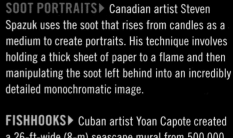

STRIKING IMAGES

▶ Fascinated by the incredible patterns that form in the blackened carbon of used wood after striking a match, Russian photographer Stanislav Aristov bends the spent matches into beautiful miniature sculptures of flowers, insects, fish, a lightbulb, and even the Eiffel Tower.

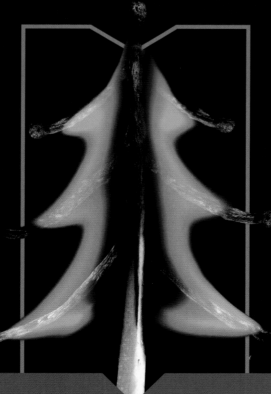

SOOT PORTRAITS▶ Canadian artist Steven Spazuk uses the soot that rises from candles as a medium to create portraits. His technique involves holding a thick sheet of paper to a flame and then manipulating the soot left behind into an incredibly detailed monochromatic image.

FISHHOOKS▶ Cuban artist Yoan Capote created a 26-ft-wide (8-m) seascape mural from 500,000 fishhooks, intertwined and nailed onto plywood. Even with the help of 30 assistants working in rotation, it took him over six months to complete.

NICE PROFIT▶ German artist Gerhard Richter's *Abstraktes Bild*, a painting described by Sotheby's as a "masterpiece of calculated chaos," sold for $34 million (£23 million) at an auction in London, England, on October 12, 2012—the highest amount ever paid for a work by a living artist. The seller was rock guitarist Eric Clapton, who had bought the colorful abstract piece as part of a set of three for $3.4 million (£2 million) in 2001.

HANGING OFFENSE▶ In December 2011, Polish art student Andrzej Sobiepan snuck one of his paintings into the National Museum in Wrocław, where it hung for three days before being noticed. Far from being angry, the museum director praised Sobiepan's initiative as a "witty artistic happening" and kept the small picture of a green leaf on display, albeit in the museum's café.

PRETTY PRINTS▶ Connecticut-based artist Kevin Van Aelst has created a series of giant fingerprints using everyday objects, including mustard, yarn, Cheetos, and cassette tapes—and each artwork is a detailed re-creation of his own fingerprints.

ANIMAL LOVER▶ Leonardo da Vinci (1452–1519) was a vegetarian and an animal rights activist who used to buy caged birds, which in Italy at that time were sold as food as well as pets, just to set them free.

MINIATURE MANHATTAN▶ Using nothing but hundreds of staples, Israeli artist Tofi Stoler built a miniature Manhattan, measuring just 4 x 14 x 20 in (10 x 35 x 50 cm) high. She has also made a model of her ukulele-playing boyfriend and re-created the scene from Francisco Goya's famous painting *The Third of May 1808*—all with metal staples.

COOKIE MOSAIC▶ The Bright School and Chattanooga Bakery of Chattanooga, Tennessee, together made a giant cookie mosaic from 16,390 Moon Pies, covering nearly 1,360 sq ft (126 sq m).

Ripley's **Believe It or Not!**®
www.ripleybooks.com

CHAIN DOGS

▶ Israeli artist Nirit Levav Packer has created a series of life-sized dog sculptures from discarded bicycle chains. Inspired after seeing chains, gears, and pedals being thrown away at her son's bicycle store, she now scours garages and bike shops across Tel Aviv for suitable parts before soldering them into place. Her chain dog sculptures, which include greyhounds, poodles, a cocker spaniel, an Afghan hound, and a Rottweiller, sell for up to $10,000 each.

NIGHT SHIFT▶ French artist Anne-Louis Girodet (1767–1824) was at his most creative at night. In order to see in the dark, he would light as many as 40 candles on the brim of his hat. He determined his fee according to the number of candles burned while painting the picture.

TEA QUEEN▶ English artist Andy Brown created a portrait of Queen Elizabeth II by stitching together 1,000 used tea bags.

CARPET FLUFF▶ Brazilian artist Tonico Lemos Auad made his name by fashioning sculptures of squirrels, lions, and cats out of pieces of carpet fluff.

CHAIN SMOKER▶ U.S. artist Jackson Pollock (1912–56) would often paint with a cigarette hanging from his lips. He used dropped cigarette ash in some of his greatest works to add texture.

NAILED IT!

▶ British artist Marcus Levine creates stunning pictures of the human body by hammering up to 50,000 metal nails into wooden boards. By varying the height and distance of the nails and rotating their heads, he can achieve different tones to give the overall effect of a pencil or charcoal drawing.

MINI MAGIC

Artist Ian Cook has more fun than should be legal, spending his days messing around with toy cars and pots of paint. When he composes one of his original artworks, instead of applying paint to the canvas with brushes, he uses remote-controlled toy cars. For bigger pieces, he has painted with real cars, motorbikes, go-karts, and even a six-ton truck!

Ian, from Birmingham, England, discovered his unique style after a trip to Latvia, where he was struck by the sheer diversity of cars. Afterward, his girlfriend of the time bought him a remote-controlled toy car, warning him not to take it down to his art studio or it would be ruined. So naturally that was the first thing he did!

At Ripley's we were so impressed with Ian's finished artwork that we bought it! The Ripley's Believe it or Not! Odditorium in London, England, displays the unique piece as part of a special multimedia exhibit showing the painting and how it was created.

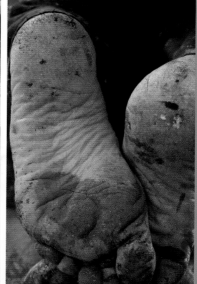

GUMSHOES

▶ Israeli designer Kobi Levi creates handmade women's high-heeled shoes in quirky sculptured shapes—including a partly peeled banana, a slingshot, a sticking-out tongue, a shark, an elephant, and sneakers with fake chewing-gum heels—that sell for more than $2,000 a pair.

MILK FABRIC ▶ A young German designer with a passion for fashion and a degree in biology has combined the two to create a range of clothes made out of milk. Anke Domaske discovered a way of mixing powdered organic milk with other ingredients to weave a special fabric for her Qmilch line.

ROTTEN TOOTH ▶ Dr. Michael Zuk, a dentist from Red Deer, Canada, paid $31,000 in 2011 for former Beatle John Lennon's rotten molar tooth that had been extracted in the 1960s.

BOSS SILENCED ▶ Shortly after welcoming Sir Paul McCartney on stage at the 2012 Hard Rock Calling festival in Hyde Park, London, England, Bruce Springsteen and 80,000 fans were silenced when the concert was cut short for breaching a council late-night noise curfew. Springsteen's three-hour gig was supposed to have finished at 10.15 p.m. but when it overran to 10.38—eight minutes beyond the curfew—officials pulled the plug.

LITTLE FEET ▶ K.B. Shivshankar displays more than 170 homemade pairs of miniature shoes, ranging from stiletto heels to gum boots, in his shoe shop in Bangalore, India. A cobbler by trade, he began making miniature shoes with the leftover materials and can handcraft a pair in just an hour. The smallest pair in his collection is 0.7 in (1.75 cm) long and the largest is 2 in (5 cm).

▶ THE HOWLING NOISE MADE BY CHEWBACCA IN STAR WARS CAME FROM AN ANGRY CAMEL. ◀

TV BANNED ▶ Bhutan was the last nation in the world to have television—as recently as 1999. Previously, it was banned, but then Bhutan's rulers decided that the country should be less isolated.

GRASS SHOES ▶ Australian footwear company KUSA has launched a range of flip-flops with fake turf stitched into the soles to give the wearer the experience of walking barefooted on grass.

OLDEST CLOWN ▶ Floyd Creekmore from Billings, Montana, was still performing as Creeky the Clown at age 95, making him the world's oldest clown. He has been entertaining crowds at fairs and rodeos since he was ten but it was not until 1981 that the former rancher became a full-time clown, in which guise he often performs with his grandson Tom McCraw.

GIANT DRUMSTICKS ▶ A concert at the Warren Amphitheater, Ohio, unveiled two 900-lb (408-kg) drumsticks carved from poplar logs in honor of hometown boy Dave Grohl, frontman of the Foo Fighters and formerly drummer with Nirvana. The giant drumsticks were engraved with feathers to represent Grohl's tattoos.

ROYAL UNDERPANTS ▶ A large pair of silk bloomers worn by Queen Victoria of England more than 100 years ago sold at an auction in Edinburgh, Scotland, in 2011 for nearly $15,000.

ABBA TRIBUTE ▶ On November 17, 2011, at Kew Primary School in Melbourne, Australia, 368 children turned into "dancing queens" to set a new record for the largest gathering of Abba impersonators.

FERMENTED FASHION

▶ Scientists from the University of Western Australia have teamed up with designer Donna Franklin to create the world's first dress made from red wine. By adding bacteria to the wine, it ferments into vinegar and a thin, cottonlike microbial skin gradually forms on the surface. The skin is then harvested and dried on an inflated mannequin, where it shrinks to fit. When the dummy is deflated, the seamless garment retains the body's shape and is ready to wear like a second skin.

HEALTHY PROFIT▶ A chipped 15th-century Ming Dynasty rice bowl, bought for just £65 ($100) in 1948 by a London collector, sold at a U.K. auction in 2012 for £1.6 million ($2.5 million).

BUILDER'S BLUNDER▶ "Parachuting Rat," a valuable piece of street art by British graffiti artist Banksy, was destroyed when a builder in Melbourne, Australia, drilled a hole through it to install a bathroom pipe.

CARDBOARD ARCADE▶ At his father's shop in Los Angeles, California, nine-year-old Caine Monroy built his own games arcade out of cardboard—complete with a range of games, prize displays, a security system, and one-month fun passes. Filmmaker Nirvan Mullick was so captivated by Caine's creation that he made a short movie about it, and a flash mob organized on Facebook led to hundreds of people lining up at the arcade to play the homemade games.

SPANISH STEPS
▶ Walking along a street in Madrid, a woman is dwarfed by a giant shoe figure, which was part of a 2012 exhibition called *Shoe Street Art*, designed to promote Spanish footwear.

LIVING WALL

▶ For his *Living Wall* series, Russian street artist Nikita Nomerz makes the country's derelict structures come alive by adding facial features. He has painted eyes and a nose on to this crumbling wall and given it white spray cans for teeth. He has also painted water towers to make it look as if they're laughing and put faces on dilapidated buildings, using the broken windows as eyes.

JUBILEE YARN▶ Great-grandmother Sheila Carter from Southampton, England, spent over 500 hours and used 4,500 ft (1,372 m) of yarn knitting her own version of the Diamond Jubilee of Queen Elizabeth II. She used an estimated 1.8 million stitches for her royal tribute, the centerpiece of which was a 3.3-ft-long (1-m) woolen barge carrying woolen likenesses of the royal family along London's River Thames toward a woolen Tower Bridge. In 2011, she had knitted a 3-ft (0.9-m) wedding cake with woolen figures of Prince William and Catherine Middleton on top.

MARMITE NATIVITY▶ Nathan Wyburn, an art student from Ebbw Vale, Wales, created a Nativity scene from 120 slices of toast coated with Marmite savory spread. His Marmite portfolio also includes portraits of Simon Cowell, Amy Winehouse, and Australian-born entertainer Rolf Harris.

DREAM CAR▶ Unable to afford the real Ferrari that he had always wanted, Chris Smart of Hampshire, England, settled for a highly realistic one that he painted on his garage door instead.

COFFEE CREATION▶ In June 2012, Russian sculptor Arkady Kim used 397 lb (180 kg) of coffee beans to produce the world's biggest coffee bean painting. Titled *Awakening*, it measured 323 sq ft (30 sq m), took two weeks to create, and was made from around one million coffee beans.

JUST A-MAZE-ING▶ Japanese artist Motoi Yamamoto creates vast intricate mazes made entirely of salt. He works by filling a plastic bottle, usually used for machine oil, with white salt and then sprinkling it on the floor. Some of his larger designs can take him up to two weeks, working 14 hours a day.

GOLD RUSH Visitors to an art gallery in Bangkok, Thailand, were challenged to search through *Sickness*, an installation filled with knee-deep yarn, in the hope of finding ten gold necklaces worth hundreds of dollars. The necklaces had been planted there by the artist, Surasi Kusolwong. Anyone who found a necklace was permitted to keep it.

CLOSE-KNIT COMMUNITY A team of more than 50 knitters from Poole, England, worked for nine months to produce a 10-ft-tall (3-m) Christmas tree consisting of 1,200 individual 8-in (20-cm) green woolen squares. They hung the squares on a metal frame and completed the tree with the addition of 200 knitted decorations, including Santas, snowmen, and reindeer.

CLAY FIGURES Using around 30 tons of clay, British sculptor Antony Gormley encouraged ordinary people to create 40,000 small terracotta humanoid figures for his piece *Field for the British Isles*. It took five days to position the characters when they were exhibited at Barrington Court, Somerset, England, in 2012.

PICTURE DIARY Angie Stevens of Swansea, Wales, drew a picture of her son Gruff almost every day for the first two years of his life—a total of more than 700 drawings—and she's still going. Doodlemum, as Angie is known, sketches a picture each evening to document things that happened to Gruff and the rest of her family that day.

SATELLITE IMAGES German artist David Hanauer created a line of elaborately patterned rugs based on satellite imagery of Earth. Inspired by the uniform layout of the streets of Las Vegas, Nevada, he used aerial images from Google Earth as prints for his modern Persian carpets, mirroring the images in four directions to give the rugs the familiar symmetrical Persian look.

SILENT PROTEST In July 2012, St. Petersburg artist Pyotr Pavlensky sewed his mouth shut with thin red string in a special performance to protest against the Russian trial of three women from the Pussy Riot punk group.

GREAT STINK A 13-ft-high (4-m) sculpture of a nose, *The Great Stink*, appeared on a bridge in London, England, in August 2012. It was promoting an exhibition to remember the terrible stench of untreated waste in the summer of 1858, which led to new laws being introduced to clean up the British capital.

FALLEN HEROES

▶ *It looks as though Ernie has fallen upon hard times, but the depiction of the* Sesame Street *character as a down-and-out is all part of a German art exhibition,* Broken Heroes, *by Patricia Waller. Her series of hand-crocheted, childhood iconic figures in peril also features Winnie the Pooh as a suicide victim, Spider-Man trapped in his own web, and Superman meeting his death by flying into a wall.*

INDEX

ACKNOWLEDGMENTS

Cover (l) Jeremy Telford; **6–7** Chooo-San/Rex Features; **8** Splash News; **9** (t/l) Cassander Eeftinck Schattenkerk, (b) Christopher Boffoli; **10** M & Y Agency Ltd/Rex Features; **11** (t) Vat19.com, (b) Reuters/Sheng Li; **12** Photographer Hal; **13** (sp) © JackF - Fotolia.com, (t/l, b/l) joce-barbiemamuse.com, (t/r) KeystoneUSA-ZUMA/Rex Features, © Corbis; **14** Solent News; **15** Reuters/Andrew Burton; **16** (t/l, t/r, c, r, b/r) Gillian Bell, Deadbright.com/Miss Cakehead, (b/l) Sarah Hardy Cakes sarahhardycakes.co.uk/Miss Cakehead; **17** Gillian Bell, Deadbright.com/Miss Cakehead; **18** (t) © Kurt Perschke/www.redballproject.com, (b/r) © Bert Folsom - Fotolia.com; **19** (c, t/l, t/r) © Kurt Perschke/www.redballproject.com, (b) Felipe Dana/AP/Press Association Images, (b/r) Marcos De Paula/DPA/Press Association Images; **20–21** Jeremy Telford; **22** (t) Ramon Bruin, (b) Freya Jobbins/Rex Features; **23** Getty Images; **24** Seth Wenig/AP/Press Association Images; **25** (t) Ben Milne, (b) Faye Halliday; **26** Sell Your Photo; **27** (t, c) Nirit Levav, (b) Marcus Levine; **30** Kobi Levi; **31** (c) Ray Scott, (b) Bewley Shaylor; **32** (t, b) Nikita Nomerz/Rex Features, (t/r) Reuters/Paul Hanna; **33** Getty Images; **Back cover** Vat19.com

Key: t = top, b = bottom, c = center, l = left, r = right, sp = single page, dp = double page

All other photos are from Ripley Entertainment Inc.
Every attempt has been made to acknowledge correctly and contact copyright holders and we apologize in advance
for any unintentional errors or omissions, which will be corrected in future editions.